Given Taiwan's distinctive history, its capital ...
ing hodgepodge of Chinese a
constantly posts a thorough i
unique to Taipei. Apart from a
actively advocating cycling as
many, Taipei's diversity is best
alleyways of Dadaocheng and
tains that border the city in the ... ... people, the city
is always warm and welcoming to visitors from around the world,
whether you're a foodie, an art lover, or a history buff.

CW00665475

CITIx60: Taipei explores this colourful capital through the eyes of
60 creative stars. Together, they take you on a journey through the
best in architecture, art spaces, shopping, cuisine and entertainment. This guide will lead you on an authentic tour of Taipei that
gets to the heart of what locals love most about their city.

Contents

Before You Go

BASIC INFO

Currency
New Taiwan dollar (TWD/NT$)
Exchange rate: US$3.3 : NT$100 : €3.1

Time zone
GMT +8
Taiwan does not observe DST.

Dialling
International calling: +886
Citywide: 2

Weather (avg. temperature range)
Spring (Mar-May): 14-28°C / 57-82°F
Summer (Jun-Aug): 23-33°C / 73-91°F
Autumn (Sep-Nov): 17-26°C / 63-79°F
Winter (Dec-Feb): 10-20°C / 50-68°F

USEFUL WEBSITES

Metro Taipei
english.metro.taipei

YouBike
taipei.youbike.com.tw

EMERGENCY CALLS

Ambulance & fire brigade
119

Police
110

Emergency call for bad cell phone reception
112

Representative offices
Japan   +886 2 2713 8000
S. Korea   +886 2 2758 8320
France   +886 2 3518 5151
Germany   +886 2 8722 2800
UK   +886 2 8758 2088
US   +886 2 2162 2000

AIRPORT EXPRESS TRANSFER

Taoyuan International Airport (TPE) <-> Taipei Main Station (Taoyuan Airport Line Express Train)
Trains / Journey: every 15 mins / 35 mins
From TPE – 0612-2244
From Taipei Main Station – 0600-2258
One-way: NT$160
www.tymetro.com.tw

Taipei Songshan Airport (TSA) <-> Taipei Main Station (Metro Taipei)
Trains / Journey: every 4-12 mins / 25 mins
From TSA – 0602-0025
From Taipei Main Station – 0600-0035
(Change @Zhongxiao Fuxing Station)
One-way: NT$25
english.metro.taipei

PUBLIC TRANSPORT IN TAIPEI

Rail / High Speed Rail
Metro
Bus
Bike
Taxi

Means of Payment
EasyCard
Cash
Credit cards

Travels with EasyCard enjoy a 20% discount over token fare on each MRT trip. Only railways accept credit card payments.

PUBLIC HOLIDAYS

January	1 New Year's Day
February	Chinese New Year*, 28 Peace Memorial Day
April	4 Children's Day, 5 Tomb Sweeping Day
May	1 Labour Day, Dragon Boat Festival*
October	Mid-Autumn Festival*, 10 National Day

Holidays* observe Chinese calendars and vary by year. Shops are likely to be closed and public services may suspend during Chinese New Year. If a holiday falls on a weekend, the closest weekday becomes a 'substitute' day.

FESTIVALS / EVENTS

February
Taipei International Book Exhibition
www.tibe.org.tw

March
Taipei Literature Festival (Through May)
FB: @tlfwh
Wonder Foto Day
www.wonderfoto.com

April
Spring Wave Music and Art Festival
www.spring-wave.com

May
Young Designers' Exhibition
www.yodex.com.tw

June
Taipei Film Festival (Through July)
www.taipeiff.taipei

July
Taipei Children's Arts Festival (Through August)
www.taipeicaf.org

August
Taipei Fringe Festival (Through September)
www.taipeifringe.org

September
Taiwan Designers' Week (Through October)
www.designersweek.tw
Taipei Arts Festival (Through October)
www.taipeifestival.org
Taipei Biennial
www.taipeibiennial.org

October
Nuit Blanche
nuitblanche.taipei

November
Digital Art Festival
www.dac.tw/daf

Event days vary by year. Please check for
updates online.

UNUSUAL OUTINGS

Experience Tea Tours
www.taipeitea.com.tw/teach.php

Meditation @Dharma Drum Mountain Centre
ncm.ddm.org.tw (CN only)

Taipei basin, Tea culture & night scenery
english.gondola.taipei

Nature/Culture Walks
www.taiwanwalks.com
www.taipei-walkingtour.tw

Inspired by Unseen Tours
www.hiddentaipei.org

SMARTPHONE APP

Real-time traffic & travel planner
Go! Taipei Metro, Citymapper

Dictionary, document reader & merged search
Pleco Chinese Dictionary

Taiwanese cuisine guide
Eat Drink Taiwan

REGULAR EXPENSES

Craft coffee
NT$120

Domestic / international mail (postcards)
NT$2.5 / NT$6-12

Gratuities
Taiwan has no tipping culture. However, fine
dining restaurants may add a 10-15% gratuity
to the bill.

Count to 10

What makes Taipei so special?

Illustrations by Guillaume Kashima aka Funny Fun

The resourceful land of Taiwan is abound with fine produce, underpinning a rich gastronomic heritage and quality mementos available across town. From newfangled cultural programmes to vibrant night markets, exploring the city is both relaxing and energising for the mind and body. Whether you're here for a day or a week, see what Taipei creative class considers an essential to-do list.

Welcome to Taipei

CLOUD GATE DANCE THEATRE

1

Performing Arts

Modern dance in search of Taiwanese roots
Cloud Gate (#21) & Cloud Gate 2

Celebrate profound tranquility
Legend Lin Dance Theatre
www.legend-lin.org.tw

Aboriginal music & dance legacy
Formosa Aboriginal Song
and Dance Troupe
fasdt.yam.org.tw

Mind-purifying percussion shows
U-Theatre, FB: @utheatre1988

Original script & newfangled theatrical language
Shakespeare's Wild Sisters Group
FB: @swsg95

Traditional Chinese Opera
TaipeiEYE, www.taipeieye.com

2

Bookshops

Yue Yue & Co.
FB: @yueyue.company

VVG Something
No. 13, Aly. 40, Ln. 181, Sec. 4, Zhongxiao East Rd., Daan

Shuijhun Bookstore
FB: @shuijhun.bookstore

Escents Bookcase
FB: @escentsbooks

JXJ Books
FB: @jxjbooks

Zeelandia Travel & Books
FB: @zeelandiabookshop

boven Magazine Library (#13)
FB: @boven437

3

Specialties made from local ingredients

Pineapple shortcake
SunnyHills Flagship Store
www.sunnyhills.com.tw

Specialty sauces & dried fruits
PEKOE, *FB: @PEKOE.TW*

Rice & camellia honey
Green-in-hand
www.greeninhand.com

Camellia oil
Cha Tzu Tang, *www.chatzutang.com*

Oolong tea
Wolf Tea
wolftea.com

Craft beer
Sambar Brewing
FB: @sambarbrewing

4

Mementos

Handmade herbal soap
Yuan Soap
www.taiwansoap.com.tw

Movable types
Ri Xing Type Foundry (#31)
FB: @rixingtypefoundry

Age-old stationery
Darenxiaoxue
FB: @darenxiaoxue

Printed fabric inspired by local scenery
inBlooom
www.inblooom.com

Local eyewear brand
Classico
FB: @2012classico

5
Modern Taipei Customs

Sip bubble tea
Chingshin, www.chingshin.tw

Watch midnight fish trades
Commadeon Fish Market
Xiao 1st Rd., Ren-ai, Keelung City

Draw divisination lots
Lungshan Temple (#2)

Seek blessings & show reverence
Hsing Tian Kong, www.ht.org.tw

Commute on a motorbike
Wherever you go in the city

Rummage in new releases through the night
Eslite Dunnan Store
FB: @eslite.dunnan.bookstore

Read comics till the small hours, and sleep next to them
QTime
No. 32, Sec. 1, Chengde Rd., Datong

6
Local Snacks

Luobo Si Bing (Radish Cakes)
Wenzhou Jie Luobo Si Bing Daren
No. 186-1, Sec. 1, Heping E. Rd., Da'an

Pepper Meat Bun
Raohe Street Night Market
Raohe St., Songshan

Gua Bao (Steamed Bun Sandwiches)
Lan Jia Gua Bao
No. 3, Aly. 8, Ln. 316, Roosevelt Rd., Zhongzheng

Yan Su Ji (Salted Crispy Chicken)
Xiongdi Yan Su Ji
www.screendoorrestaurant.com

Cong Zhua Bing (Scallion Pancakes)
Linjia Cong Zhua Bing
No. 8, Ln. 235, Zhongzheng Rd., Shilin

Grilled Sausages
Tonghua Night Market
Linjiang St., Da'an

7
Typical Breakfast Combos

Soy Milk & Hot Buns
Da San Yuan Doujiang Dian
No. 233, Ningbo W. St., Zhongzheng

French Toast
Chengenzhaocha
No. 7, Ln. 391, Zhuangjing Rd., Xinyi

Lurou Fan (Braised Pork Rice)
Yuan Huan Lurou Fan Rou Geng
FB: @store.fruit

Ba-wan (Huge Pork Dumpling)
A Cai Zhanghua Ba Wan
No. 13, Ln. 21, Longjiang Rd., Zhongshan

Dang Bing (Egg Crêpe)
Wei Ding Dan Bing
No. 3, Ln. 21, Longjiang Rd., Zhongshan

Scallion pancake
Mei & Mei
www.mam.com.tw

8

Midnight Feed

Chilled Noodles
Chen's Noodles in Sauce
*No. 29, Ln. 123, Sec. 5, Nanjing E. Rd.,
Songshan*

Pan-fried Milkfish Belly
Ah Tsai Milkfish
No. 53, Neijiang St., Wanhua

Beef noodles
Lin Tung Fong Beef Noodles
No. 274 Sec. 2, Bade Rd., Zhongshan

Fresh Seafood
Xun Xian Shengmeng Huo Haixian
*No. 80, Ln. 300, Sec. 2, Bade Rd.,
Zhongshan*

Spicy Hotpot
Chan Ji Hot Pots Lab.
*No. 178, Sec. 2, Nanjing E. Rd.,
Zhongshan*

From ice-cream to Japanese oden
7-Eleven Convenient Stores

9

Vegetarian Delights

Yang Ming Spring Restaurant
ymspring.com.tw

Sankansoubo Japanese Cuisine
www.sankansoubo.com.tw

About Animals (#40)
FB: @aboutanimalszr

Naked Food
nkdfood.delicioustaipei.com

URBN Culture
FB: @urbnculture

The Green Room
FB: @thegreenroomtpe

Mori Vegan Ice-cream
FB: @MORIVegan

10

Taiwanese Café Culture

Nordic coffee
Fika Fika Cafe, *FB: @FikaFikaCafe*

Standing room only
COFFEE : STAND UP
FB: @coffeestandup

Homemade cakes
Afterhours Café,
FB: @afterhourscafe

Award-winning barista at helm
GABEE., *FB: GABEE.*

Patio & irregular mini-flea market
COSTUMICE CAFÉ
FB: @costumice.cafe

Cold brews & traditional desserts
Fong Da Coffee
No. 42, ChengDou Rd., Wanhua

Café & vinyl music
BEANS & BEATS Coffee & Records
FB: @beansnbeats

Icon Index

 Opening hours

 Admission

 Address

 Facebook

 Contact

 Website

 Remarks

 Scan QR codes to access Google Maps and discover the area around each destination. Internet connection required.

60x60

60 Local Creatives x 60 Hotspots

From vast cityscapes to the tiniest glimpses of everyday exchanges, there's always something to provoke your imagination. 60X60 points you to 60 haunts where 60 arbiters of taste cut their teeth.

Landmarks & Architecture — SPOTS · 01 – 12 ●

Embodying contrasting cultures, the city's historic builds attest to Taiwan's turbulent past. Libraries or school, modern architectures are habitually designed with nature in mind.

Cultural & Art Spaces — SPOTS · 13 – 24 ●

Resided in deserted lanes, alleys and old factory complexes, exhibition and performance spaces of different sizes play a major part in developing a vibrant cultural and art scene.

Markets & Shops — SPOTS · 25 – 36 ●

Experience day-to-day Taipei by going to traditional markets. Bring home unique crafts, designs and goods made from local produce along with fond memories.

Restaurants & Cafés — SPOTS · 37 – 48 ●

Taipei's artisan coffee is known for its quality blends and brews as well as characterful store spaces. Be it Taiwanese or Western cuisine, local and seasonal food guarantees good taste.

Nightlife — SPOTS · 49 – 60 ●

There are a million ways to spend a night in Taipei. Enjoy the city's night view on Yangming Mountain, then hit the bar for local craft beers, party at premium clubs or devour street eats.

Landmarks & Architecture

Majestic temples, colonial heritage and sleek modern builds

Taipei's city planning is a vestige of its political past. Much like Tokyo, the address system goes through fine subdivisions. The hierarchy of sections, lanes and alleys indexed by numbers makes for easy navigation, especially for those who do not read Chinese. Xinyi (fidelity), Bade (eight virtues), Nanjing, Chongqing – the naming of boulevards after Chinese values and cities in 1947 denotes the start of an era under the Republic of China.

The Japanese rulers left behind a cluster of government buildings and residence. Some are strictly Japanese, such as the houses on Qidong Street (#7), and others their interpretation of Western architecture, which are also prevalent in Japan at the time. One example is The Office of the President (*No. 122, Sec. 1, Chongqing S. Rd., Zhongzheng*), which was built in 1919 as the Governor's Office and is still in use today, forming the largest group of Japanese-built Western style architecture in the world.

Entering the 21st century, Taipei 101 (*www.taipei-101.com.tw*) becomes the new face of the city. Bringing international spotlight to Taipei, architect C.Y. Lee's postmodern design retains Eastern motifs. His attempt to breathe new life into contemporary architecture sets the tone for later projects in the city. Take a look at Shih Chien University (#3) and the tranquil Water-Moon Monastery (*No. 89, Ln. 65, Daye Rd., Beitou*). Both Kris Yao Artech designs are considered essentially Taiwanese.

Feng, Yu
Founder, IF OFFICE

Formerly the creative and artistic director of magazines *PPAPER* and *2535*, Feng Yu runs a full-service design house, and gives design seminars at organisations and institutes.

National Palace Museum
P.014

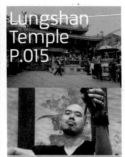

Lungshan Temple
P.015

Muh Chen
Director, Grass Jelly

Muh Chen likes to take on challenges. Apart from music videos and advertisements, he is always ready to carry forward his creativity to make something new.

Ho, Ting-an
Art director & graphic designer

Ho Ting-an set up STUDIO 411 in 2014. Current practice spans branding designs and art-direction for music videos and live shows. His motion graphics appeared in the Venice Biennale.

College of Design @ SCU
P.016

Andrew Wong
Onion Design Associates

Movies, hiking, cats and Stephen Chow's comedies are all Andrew Wong's favourites next to design. He still dreams of becoming a rocker and teaches at Xue Xue Institute in real life.

Treasure Hill
P.017

Koo Chen-fu Memorial Library
P.018

Mike He
Founder, Pistacchi Design

With a special brand of hilarity, I am also a serious food lover. I draw ideas from my travels and delicious food. I am thrilled to show you my second home city, where east and west meet.

Lee, Chi
Founder, Lightance

Taiwanese native Lee Chi's designs integrate plants into spaces. Through the internet, Lee strives to grasp how the world works and shape human brains.

Taipei Botanical Garden
P.020

Whooli Chen
Illustrator

Whooli Chen loves cat as much as she loves words and pictures, in one place or otherwise. She is one half of Sometime-else Practice, and the illustrator of CITIx60 Taipei's map jacket.

Elephant Mountain Hiking Trail
P.022

Riin
Musician & writer

Riin is a founding member and vocalist of electronic pop trio The Girl and The Robots. She also writes music and short stories.

Kair Chen
Photographer

Kair Chen is a freelance photographer. Through the lens, he resonates with the world. He simply loves to live a life that is free of constraints.

Qidong St. Japanese Houses
P.021

Dihua Street
P.023

Baboo
Theatre director

Baboo has been involved in stage direction and released 23 productions since 1997. He is now a director-in-residence at Shakespeare's Wild Sisters Group.

Beitou Public Library
P.026

HereThere Studio
Multimedia studio

HereThere is where musical artists can complete their album production from start to finish. Our practice combines music recording and graphic design.

Sihow Yah
Co-founder, Sense30

An advocate of bicycle fashion, Sihow Yah started vintage bike brand Sense30 with a goal to make cycling an essential part of urban dwellers' daily lives.

National Theater and Concert Hall
P.024

Taipei Riverside Bikeways
P.027

1 National Palace Museum

Map V, P.110

The National Palace Museum boasts one of the world's largest and finest collection of ancient Chinese artefacts and artworks. At the various themed galleries, visitors will come face to face with Shang- and Zhou-dynasty bronze vessels, notable calligraphic work from Tang China, as well as Song-era porcelain and paintings that are all over a thousand years old. At 16 hectares, the museum itself is a grand work of art modelled after Beijing's Forbidden City. After your visit, stroll around the scenic gardens to take in the sense of peace that marks traditional Chinese landscape design.

🕐 0830–1830 (Su–Th), –2100 (F–Sa) 💲 NT$250/150
🏠 No. 221, Sec. 2, Zhishan Rd., Shilin
📞 +886 2 2881 2021
URL www.npm.gov.tw

"Although Ru ware is said to be the museum's main draw, I suggest you check out their Ding ware collection (also from Song dynasty, 960–1127)."

– Feng Yu, IF OFFICE

2 Lungshan Temple
Map A, P.102

Founded in 1738, Lungshan Temple snuggles in Wanhua District, once the epicentre of urban culture in Taipei. Since its founding, the temple has acted as the axis of religious life as well as a place to discuss community affairs and settle disputes. Designed as a south-facing courtyard complex, Lungshan Temple is an excellent example of classic Taiwanese architecture and craftsmanship – its exquisite pair of bronze dragon columns at the entrance are truly one of their kind. Take time to appreciate the meticulous wood work, effigies and paintings that fill the roofs and halls.

🕐 0600-2200 daily
🏠 No. 211, Guangzhou St., Wanhua
📞 +886 2 2302 5162
🌐 www.lungshan.org.tw

"*The incense smoke may cause irritation of the eyes, and the temple is always packed, so do watch out for your belongings.*"

– Muh Chen, Grass Jelly

3 College of Design @Shih Chien University
Map Y, P.111

Occupying a pint-sized site in the Zhongshan District, the College of Design complex at the southern edge of Shih Chien University campus floats over an open courtyard that creates an airy and pleasant entrance to the school. Taiwanese architect Kris Yao's vision was to break away from building a conventional enclosed facility and connect the neighbouring community with two interlocking triangular blocks, fashionably dressed in matt grey concrete, steel and glass. Aluminium panels work as sunshades and add a tectonic rhythm to the south and east walls. Interactions with light project an ever-changing facade.

🏠 No. 70, Dazhi St., Zhongshan
📞 +886 2 2538 1111
🌐 www.scdesign.usc.edu.tw

"I still remember how I was overawed when I passed into the building. It won't take long to walk through the site but the clever design justifies its many awards."

– Ho Ting-an

4 Treasure Hill

Map O, P.109

Perched on a hill next to the Xindian River is Treasure Hill, a small art village with a unique historic past. Once home to Kuomingtang soldiers and their families upon their arrival in Taiwan in the 1940s and slated to be demolished decades later after the residents left, the illegally-built barracks were saved by protestors, which eventually led to its preservation. Officially made part of the Taipei Artist Village, the site is now a community of creative workshops, exhibition space, and a cute tiny café awaiting you to snake around through the narrow alleyways.

🕐 1100–2200 (Tu–Su), exhibition –1800
🏠 Ln. 230, Sec. 3, Tingzhou Rd., Zhongzheng
📞 +886 2 2364 5313
URL www.artistvillage.org

"Slow your pace up the meandering stairs and anticipate the ethereal scenes to come into view."

– Andrew Wong, Onion Design Associates

5 Koo Chen-fu Memorial Library

Map K, P.107

Designed by Japanese architect Toyo Ito, Koo Chen-fu Memorial Library is the new landmark of National Taiwan University. Over 88 white columns support the ceiling of the library and formed 130 skylight punctures that bring light right across the space. Together with floor-to-ceiling windows, shadow play gives alternating patterns throughout the day, recreating more or less a forested landscape within the walls. The open space is divided by curved bamboo bookshelves, co-produced with local bamboo artist Liu Wen-huang.

🕑 0820–2100 (M–F), 0900– (Sa), 0900–1700 (Su)
🏠 No. 1, Sec. 4, Roosevelt Rd., Da'an
📞 +886 2 3366 8300
🔗 web.lib.ntu.edu.tw/koolib
🖉 Closes on Sundays during summer and winter holidays.

"The light shafts help illuminate the space and bring library users closer to nature."

– Mike He, Pistacchi Design

6   Taipei Botanical Garden
Map A, P.102

Located in Taipei's downtown, a quick walk through Taipei's Botanical Garden is a fine way to break out of the city's hustle and bustle. Founded in 1921, this nine-hectare green space dates back to 1897 when the Japanese colonial government set up a gardening institute on the premises. The scene of lotus flowers covering the lake is a popular sight in summer, but locals come round the year to admire the impressive collection of tropical plants. If you like history and crafts, The National Museum of History and the National Taiwan Craft Research and Development Institute are just around the corner.

🕑 0530-2200 daily
🏠 No. 53, Nanhai Rd., Zhongzheng
📞 +886 2 2303 9978 (ext. 1420)
🔗 tpbg.tfri.gov.tw

"The nearby Guling Street is teeming with show venues, used furniture shops and restaurants with a cultural edge, a perfect respite and area for new ideas."
– Lee Chi, Lightance

7 Qidong Street Japanese Houses

Map F, P.105

Taiwan's colonisation by the Japanese from 1895 to 1945 left behind various legacies, one of them being some ten houses on Qidong Street. Previously known as Saiwai-cho, this area was once the home of Japanese civil servants. Thanks to the impressive craftsmanship and preservation efforts, these distinctly Japanese porches, interior spaces and gardens can still be admired today. Visit Qidong Poetry Salon, Taipei Qin Hall and Taipei Calligraphy Institute, all re-purposed from the houses and open to the public.

🏠 Ln. 53, Qidong St., Zhongzheng
🔗 Qidong Poetry Salon: poeticleap.moc.gov.tw, Taipei Qin Hall: www.taipeiqinhall.com

"Remember to wear socks as shoes are not allowed indoor."

– Whooli Chen

8 Elephant Mountain Hiking Trail

Map M, P.108

Taipei's skyline is defined by Xinyi District's commercial area, and most prominently Taiwan's tallest building, Taipei 101. You can take in a panorama of the cityscape on top of Elephant Mountain. Though it's only 183 metres high, this small mountain not far from the bustling CBD has got a pleasant hiking trail where one can spot a rich variety of insects and plant species, thus a popular family destination. A moderate hike, the trail also attracts fitness lovers looking for a short run. The huge stone at the top of the mountain is an ideal photo spot, especially at sunset and during the night.

🏠 *Aly. 22, Ln. 150, Zhongqiang Park, Sec. 5, Xinyi Rd., Xinyi towards Yongchungong Park, Songshan Rd.*

"The best spot to capture Taipei 101! Visit on a weekday as you will be among crowds during weekends."

– Riin, The Girl and The Robots

9 Dihua Street
Map B, P.103

Erected in the mid-19th century, Dihua Street and the surrounding Dadaocheng neighbourhood boast a mixture of Minnan architecture, Western-style trading companies and Baroque-style facades. More than 70 historical buildings still stand and businesses run as usual on street level premises, inviting shoppers to survey the array of traditional goods sold here – Chinese medicine, spices, dried fruits, incense, temple goods and crafts, to name a few. Recent renewal efforts has lured new cultural and creative ventures in the area, adding a new flow of energy to the already unique streetscape where old meets new.

🏠 Dihua St., Datong

"Check out the well preserved Japanese builds that line the old street, and things that you can cook at your place. Then watch the sun set at Dadaocheng Wharf."
— Kair Chen

10 National Theater and Concert Hall

Map A, P.103

Built as an extension to the neighbouring Chiang Kai-shek Memorial Hall in the 1980s, the National Theater and National Concert Hall parallel the palatial architecture of northern China. Despite their classical Chinese facade, the venues house a sleek and modern interior, complete with world-class acoustical spaces and performance equipment. While the two halls stage top-tier performances from ballet, symphonies to Chinese opera, the public square in between runs a robust programme of free outdoor concerts as well as dance rehearsals by youth groups.

🏠 No. 21-1, Chungshan S. Rd., Zhongzheng
📞 +886 2 3393 9888
URL npac-ntch.org
🔗 Online ticketing: www.artsticket.com.tw

"The grandeur of its classic Chinese exterior and its western proscenium arch stage make it a mandatory stop for visitors from around the world."

– Baboo, Shakespeare's Wild Sisters Group

11 Beitou Public Library
Map R, P.110

Sitting on a tree-hugged site at the heart of Beitou Park, this public library branch aims to foster a stronger bond between local citizens and the nature, with green concepts in mind. Like a giant log cabin with an expansive terrace, the structure is designed to minimise reliance on artificial lighting and air-conditioning. The library's roof garden also recycles rainwater for reuse. If this cannot take you away from the daily grind, hit one of the inexpensive hot spring bathhouses in the area.

🕐 0900-1700 (Su-M), 0830-2100 (Tu-Sa)
🏠 No. 251, Guangming Rd., Beitou
📞 +886 2 2897 7682
🔗 Closes monthly first Thursdays and public holidays

"Arrange an overnight trip to spare time for the Hot Spring Museum and Thermal Valley. Also visit Sheme House nearby, which is a café converted from a barn."
– HereThere Studio

12 Taipei Riverside Bikeways
Map AA, P.111

Biking along the riverside is one of the best ways to experience leisure Taipei. Used to be dirty and polluted, the Tamsui and Keelung Rivers now offer a scenic view to bikers thanks to city government's cleansing efforts. Simply rent a bike from the city's public bikeshare system, YouBike, outside MRT stations and take in the cityscape before making your way to the Keelung Riverside Bike Trail via Dajia Park. If you have a bit more time, follow the Tamsui Trail from downtown Taipei towards Tamsui. On this route, you'll pass by Guandu Nature Park and end at Tamsui Old Street, known for it's street food.

🏠 *Water gate No. 8, Binjiang St., Zhongshan towards Tamsui*

🔗 *www.riversidepark.taipei.gov.tw/BikePath*

"You will experience the laid-back side of Taipei along this bike lane just a stone throw away from city centre."

– Sihow Yah, Sense30

Cultural & Art Spaces

Unrivalled programmes, boutique galleries and creative conversions

A celebration of local talent, the great sense of community coupled with global ambitions set the backdrop for Taipei's burgeoning art and culture scene. Cloud Gate Dance Theater's (#21) choreography is deeply inspired by the land, society and folk culture of Taiwan. Nurturing primarily local dancers, the theatre's fusion of modern dance with Eastern aesthetics transcends cultures and mesmerised audience from around the world.

In a way, Taipei's industrial past has contributed to its present-day culture scene. An old winery cluster in city centre was transformed into Huashan 1914 Creative Park (#24), a series of multipurpose spaces that offer an incredible range of performances, exhibitions and more. One can also complete the trip with a visit to the nearby MOCA Taipei (www.mocataipei.org.tw). To catch up on local design trends and discover emerging designers, go to Songshan Cultural & Creative Park (www.songshanculturalpark.org) converted from a now-defunct cigarette factory.

The people of Taiwan love exhibitions and seminars. From the large-scale Taiwan Biennial by Taipei Fine Arts Museum (www.tfam.museum) to the smaller literary salons, you can expect an enthusiastic crowd. Head to residential neighbourhoods if you are a fan of independent galleries and cultural establishments. Lanes and alleys are where they quietly flourish. Curated by independent gallerists, spaces such as Pon Ding (#14) and boven magazine library (#13) are thus full of personalities and show just how keen Taipei creatives are carrying forward their passion.

Val Chen
Costume designer

Val Chen founded humancloning in 2014 to focus on costume design, as well as art direction for films and videos. She is also keen on product design, styling and making art.

boven
magazine
library
P.032

Pon Ding
P.033

Cheng, Hsiao-ron
Illustrator

National Taiwan University of Arts graduate Cheng Hsiao-ron's work are seen on music albums, book covers and in magazines. Her clients include Entertainment Weekly and L'Oréal.

siu siu: Lab
of Primitive
Senses
P.036

Kenyon Yeh
Founder & brand director, Esaila

Kenyon Yeh worked independently after finishing his MA Product Design at London's Kingston University. He now creates minimalist products that are made in Taiwan.

Chou, Tung-yen
Founder, Very Mainstream Studio

Graduated with a MA in Scenography from Central Saint Martins, Chou Tung-yen was awarded at World Stage Design for his theatrical production, *Emptied Memories*, in 2013.

The Red
House
P.034

Noah Cheng
CEO, Xue Xue Institute

I am a husband and a father of two. I work with a group of highly creative and dedicated people. Come to Xue Xue for a chat and learn more about what we do!

Xue Xue
Institute
P.037

Ken-tsai Lee
Graphic designer

Also an Associate Professor at National Taiwan University of Science and Technology, Ken-tsai Lee champions the use of Chinese type in design.

Beitou
Museum
P.035

Tamago Yeh
Founder, OVAL

Tamago Yeh finished graduate school at Kyoto University of Art & Design in 2012. He has published books for Akira Kobayashi in Taiwan and curated Taiwan's first typography magazine.

transpark
P.040

biaugust
Design studio

We do not only offer design, but also our experience and philosophy in life that touch the audience's heart.

Chou, Shu-yi
Choreographer

I create with my body through dance, choreography, writing and photography. I am deeply concerned about the balance of nature and ecology with art and culture.

Not Just
Library
P.038

Cloud Gate
Theater
P.041

Divooe Zein
Architect

Divooe Zein set up his namesake firm in 2002 and started an ecological architecture laboratory in UBud, Bali, in 2008. In 2014, he moved part of his experiment to siu siu – Lab of Primitive Senses.

SPOT Taipei
P.044

Paper Travel
Illustration brand

"Life is a trip without a destination, and we are each other's scenery." Paper travel is a creative project inspired by travel and trivial happenings in daily life.

Johnason Lo
Founder, JL Design

JL is the first Asian agency to have designed the visual identity and offer design consultation to the Al Jazeera TV network. JL's other clients include HBO Asia, FOX Japan, and Mercedes-Benz.

Suho Me-
morial Paper
Museum
P.042

Huashan 1914
Creative Park
P.045

13 boven magazine library
Map H, P.106

Inspired by comic book rental stores, Spencer
Chou (P.089) established boven, a library
dedicated solely to magazines. Magazine lovers
will be delighted to find its shelves packed with
more than 15,000 magazines that cover topics
ranging from lifestyle and fashion to leisure, all
selected for their refined art direction and editorial as well as insight into their subject matter.
Magazine industry figures travel far to visit this
special haunt. Don't forget to chat with Spencer
and ask him all about his collections.

🕐 1200-2200 daily 💲 Daily rate: NT$300
🏠 B1, No. 18, Aly. 5, Ln. 107, Sec. 1, Fuxing S. Rd., Da'an
📞 +886 2 2778 7526 📘 @boven437

*"Frequented by independent designers, this is where
they go when feeling burnt out in their own studios."*
– Val Chen, humancloning

14 Pon Ding
Map D, P.104

Founded by industrial designer Kenyon Yeh (p.030) and publisher Chen Yi-chiu in 2016, Pon Ding is equally parts a magazine shop, event space, art gallery and coffee shop. The ground floor stocks select international fashion and lifestyle periodicals, as well as indie publications, while furniture designed by Yeh and freshly brewed coffee invite a prolonged stay. The gallery and performance spaces upstairs stage separate monthly shows, so take the chance to view exciting work by artists from Taiwan as well as other parts of Asia.

🕐 1100–2000 (Tu–Su)
🏠 No. 6, Ln. 53, Sec. 1, Zhongshan N. Rd., Zhongshan
📞 +886 2 25377281
🔗 pon-ding.com

"Much more than a gallery with a café, Pon Ding's space design connects food, publication and art in a spontaneous and intimate fashion."

– Cheng Hsiao-ron

15 The Red House
Map A, P.102

Conceived by Japanese architect Kondo Juro, this 1908 red brick architecture features a rare cruciform structure that connects with an octagonal tower. A class III historic site, The Red House was originally a public market before repurposed as a Chinese opera theatre after WWII and currently an art and cultural hub with performing arts venues, exhibition space and a gift shop. It also hosts outdoor market at weekends to promote local arts and crafts. At night, have fun hanging out at the bars around the South Square, which has become a popular destination for Taipei's LGBT community.

🕐 1100-2130 (Tu-Th, Su), -2200 (F-Sa)
🏠 No. 10, Chengdu Rd., Wanhua
☎ +886 2 2311 9380
URL www.redhouse.org.tw

"Start your club night from behind The Red House, where the public square is densely populated with LGBT-friendly outdoors bars."

– Chou Tung-yen, Very Mainstream Studio

16 Beitou Museum
Map S, P.110

Built during Japanese colonisation in 1921, the museum was originally a luxurious hot spring hotel frequented by Japanese pilots throughout the time of WWII. The museum now holds an array of art and cultural performances and exhibitions on the indigenous people as well as Taiwanese and Japanese folk arts and artefacts, celebrating Beitou's time-honoured history as a hot spring town. Visitors can reserve tatami rooms for creative vegetarian Kaiseki meals as well.

🕙 1000–1800 (Tu–Su) 💲 NT$120/50
🏠 No. 32, Youya Rd., Beitou
URL www.beitoumuseum.org.tw
🖉 Free guided tours: 1100, 1430 (Sa–Su & P.H.)

"Enjoy a day trip away from city centre's air pollution, indulge in a hot spring and take in the beauty of old Taiwan under Japanese influence."

– Ken-tsai Lee

17 siu siu: Lab of Primitive Senses

Map W, P.111

On a hillside near Waishuangxi is siu siu, a "testing ground" for the body and mind. The mesh covering the wooden arch structure reminiscent of a greenhouse is transparent, allowing for a continual conversation with the natural surroundings from inside. siu siu is built and operated by architect Divooe Zein (P.031) and his firm, whose aim is to explore the environmental transition between urban space and natural forest. Visitors will feel immersed in the subtropical rainforest setting, surrounded by its animal and insect inhabitants. Be sure to call ahead, since they only open by appointment or for special events.

🏠 *No. 148, Sec. 3, Zhishan Rd., Shilin*
🔗 *www.siusiu.tw*

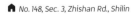

"Do make an appointment by phone or email before your visit."

– Kenyon Yeh, Esaila

⑱ Xue Xue Institute
Map AB, P.111

As technology companies make Neihu District their home, the area has become known as Taiwan's Silicon Valley. Hidden among all the glass towers in the neighbourhood is Xue Xue Institute, a centre promoting creativity and innovation. Established in 2005, Xue Xue Institute draws big names from the local creative industry for numerous events and talks.

Exhibitions of international art and design can be found on the sixth and seventh floor, while Xue Nong Foodery offers creative and authentic flavours of New Taiwanese cuisine.

🕐 *Hours & tour arrangements vary with shows*
💲 *NT$200* 🏠 *No. 207, Sec. 2, Tiding Blvd., Neihu*
📞 *+886 2 8751 6898* 🌐 *www.xuexue.tw*
🔗 *Foodery: 1000–1800 daily*

"Come early before class, especially during summer to catch the sunset over Keelung River at 6.30pm."

– Noah Cheng, Xuexue Institute

19 Not Just Library
Map L, P.108

Located in Songshan Cultural and Creative Park, Not Just Library is Taiwan's first library dedicated solely to design publications. With over 20,000 books and magazines in their collection, it's easy for design professionals and fanatics alike to spend an entire afternoon here. Acclaimed interior designer Yao Cheng-chung retains the open layout and large glass windows of the old cigarette factory, creating an unusual but welcoming setting for a library. There is a small space in the library that holds exhibitions, intermittently featuring the works of young designers and artists, and also hosts interesting talks at weekends.

- 🕙 1000–1800 (Tu–Su)
- 💲 NTS50/30/day
- 🏠 2/F, No. 133, Guangfu S. Rd., Xinyi
- 📞 +886 2 2745 8199
- URL www.boco.com.tw/notjust

"It's the reading spot for Taipei's design community. There's also a nice book café, Yue Yue & Co. nearby."

– Tamago Yeh, OVAL

20 transpark

Map I, P.107

The Minsheng Community is considered one of Taipei's most liveable neighbourhoods, with numerous parks scattered along its quiet residential, tree-lined streets. Located at the corner of one of Minsheng's residential blocks is transpark, a small exhibition and event space. With large glass windows overlooking one of the neighbourhood's parks, transpark provides a refreshing take on the "white cube" for art exhibitions. The founders of transpark have a background in film and established the space to accommodate the exhibition needs of their artist friends.

🕐 1230-2030 (Tu-Su)
🏠 No. 15, Ln. 131, Sec. 4, Minsheng E. Rd., Songshan
📘 transpark.tp

"Enjoy a moment of tranquility from the intermittent art exhibitions, seminars and drama performances here."
– biaugust

21 Cloud Gate Theater
Map Q, P.110

Founded in 1973 by Lin Hwai-min, Cloud Gate Dance Theater has gained international acclaim for its confluence of traditional Chinese and modern dance. In 2014, Cloud Gate moved into a new space in Tamsui on the outskirts of the city. Designed by Huang Sheng-yuan of Fieldoffice Architects, this organically-shaped building boasts three theatres, the largest of which has 450 seats. Visitors are able to get in touch with Cloud Gate's rich history here, particularly in the preserved remnants of its original studio, which was destroyed in a fire.

🏠 *No. 36, Ln. 6, Sec. 1, Zhongzheng Rd., Tamsui, New Taipei City*
📞 *+886 2 2629 8558*
🔗 *www.cloudgate.org.tw*

"Also get a glimpse of Taiwan's Spanish colonial past by visiting historic architecture nearby."
– Chou Shu-yi

22 Suho Memorial Paper Museum

Map E, P.104

Transformed from an ordinary narrow row in 1995, the four-storey museum is curated in memory of Chen Shu-ho and his wife, who had both spent a lifetime devoted to paper handcrafts. An absolute heaven for paper lovers, the showroom and shop on the ground floor offer a variety of paper products for sale. Exhibition spaces on the upper floors showcase different paper art and design as well as utilitarian products in Taiwan with interactive display. The museum regularly collaborates with artists for temporary exhibitions, and also offers papermaking workshops for children and adults.

🕐 0930-1630 (M-Sa), Shop: -1700 (M-Sa) 💲 NT$100
🏠 No. 68, Sec. 2, Chang'an E. Rd., Zhongshan
📞 +886 2 2507 5535
🔗 www.suhopaper.org.tw
🖋 Paper-making: 1000/1100/1400/ 1500, Family combo (1 adult + 1 child): NT$300, Single: NT$180 (incl. entrance)

"Check for current exhibitions online before your visit."
– Divooe Zein, Divooe Zein Architects

23 SPOT Taipei
Map D, P.104

Boasting a grand balcony and austere archways reminiscent of colonial houses in the American south, this previous home of US–Taiwan relations is now one of Taipei's best places for arthouse films. After nearly 20 years of abandonment, the quaint mansion was restored in 1997 to become SPOT Taipei. Run by the Taiwan Film & Culture Association, audience can attend a wide range of independent movie screenings and talks by visiting directors and have light meals at SPOT Café Lumière, which occupies the old reception room.

🕐 Café Lumière: 1000–2200 (Su–Th), –0000 (F–Sa)
🏠 No. 18, Sec. 2, Zhongshan N. Rd., Zhongshan
📞 +886 2 2511 7786 URL www.spot.org.tw
🖉 Tickets are sold on 1/F: NT$260/240/200

"Feel the presence of a special historical past in this singular architecture."

– Paper Travel

 Huashan 1914 Creative Park

Map F, P.105

At the heart of Taipei stands Huashan, formerly home to numerous sake breweries and wineries, which operated continuously from 1914 until 1987 when they fell into ruin. The old industrial grounds then became multipurpose space for various theatre groups and artists, before it transformed into the array of exhibition and art spaces, as well as restaurants and shops that it houses today. At the weekends, exhibition hungry Taipei dwellers come here to enjoy creative shows and live performances. The green space north of the Park is also a great place for picnic and is where the biennial Simple Life Festival is held.

🕐 *Hours vary with programmes and shops*
🏠 *No. 1, Sec. 1, Bade Rd., Zhongzheng*
📞 *+886 2 2358 1914*
🔲 *www.huashan1914.com*

"Enjoy light meals in the green space or head to VVG Thinking in the park for French fusion cuisine."

– Johnason Lo, JL Design

Markets & Shops

Traditional groceries, homegrown labels and curated lifestyle goods

Taipei has seen a surge in entrepreneurial spirit thanks to reasonable rent and most importantly the people's urge to bring about something better than the market currently offers. The city is filled with endless new retail shops to show for it. What these entrepreneurs share is an interest in seeking a quality way of life, and the differences in their findings can be seen in what they sell.

While shopping for handpicked items, don't forget to chat with the shop owners. Their vision and unique insight will tell something more about the brand. Go to ArtYard (*No. 67, Sec. 1, Dihua St.*) and A Design&Life Project (*No. 279, Nanjing W. Rd.*) in the historic Dadaocheng neighbourhood, which both embrace local craftsmanship. The successful chain VVG (*FB: @vvgteam*) dots the city which are all a reliable spot for some quality retail therapy. At weekends, head to Good Cho's (#28) for Simple Market, where you can shop for design goods and a wide range of locally-sourced produce.

While design stores showcase immense creativity of the younger generation, traditional marketplaces are where you can experience Taiwanese's day-to-day life. Get to know Chinese dried foods and spices at Nanmen Market (#34) and marvel at local flora at Jianguo Weekend Flower Market (#36). The spaces will be jam-packed, but the hustle and bustle is part of old markets' charm.

Chang, Chieh
Photographer

An alumni of Shih Chien University's graduate school of Communications Design, Chang Chieh questions about the future in his work.

Chenjingkai Office
P.052

Alice Wang
Product designer

Alice Wang holds a MA Design Interactions from the Royal College of Art and BA Product Design from Central Saint Martins. Her work illustrates the ironic habits that lay deep among us.

Hsin Tan
Fashion designer, tan tan

Hsin Tan set up her own fashion label tan tan in 2014.

Delicate Antique
P.050

The Town Crier
P.053

Wang, Ching-fu
Art director, Pinmo Design Studio

Wang Ching-fu draws on his experiences and daily life to create. He enjoys sunbathing and is currently a part-time lecturer of Applied Arts at Fu Jen Catholic University.

Eslite Spectrum Songyan
P.056

Finger and Toe
Multimedia studio

Director Su Sheng-yang and graphic designer Lin Show-me produce experimental motion graphics. They will tackle screenwriting next and build something up from a good story.

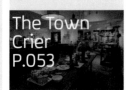

Grace Wang
CEO, VVG Group

Grace Wang fuses her life and travel experiences into management and forges VVG into a lifestyle village. VVG Something was named one of World's Most Beautiful Bookstore.

Good Cho's
P.054

Fuhe Bridge Flea Market
P.058

Yin, Tsan-yu
Type & graphic designer

A graphic design nomad fuelled by a passion for typography.

Echo Store
P.060

justfont
Type design studio

Su Wei-hsiang co-founded justfont, the online Chinese type design platform that launched the jf Jing-Shuan Font Family. He strives to stimulate Taiwanese's interests towards typography.

Firstofmay studio
Designer brand

Firstofmay is DJ Elvis and illustrator May, who integrate music and illustration as the foundation of their own brand. Their work has appeared in music festivals and album packaging.

Ri Xing Type Foundry
P.059

White Wabbit Records
P.062

Ann, Yu-chien
Architect

I am an architect, designer, former Dean of College of Design at Shih Chien University.

Yongle Fabric Market
P.064

Sim Chang
Visual artist & photographer

Sim Chang is the winner of the International Photography Awards and PX3. His work has been made part of the permanent collection of Kiyosato Photo Art Museum in Japan.

Committee of boys' day-off, *Publishing studio*

A photography project inspired by life events and travel. Zooming in on Japan, The group has published the books *Sakyoto daily day-off* and *Douou daily-day off*.

Nanmen Market
P.063

Jianguo Weekend Flower Market
P.065

25 Delicate Antique
Map K, P.107

A stark industrial space made up of bricks and iron sheets, Delicate Antique is decked with age-old furniture and homeware sleekly curated by the owner, Jin. Having worked in the music industry for years until he discovered his love for collecting vintage objects, Jin scours far and wide and brings home French display cabinets to British jewellery boxes. Thanks to his sharp eyes for found objects and focus to showcase "approachable works of art", this stripped down space attracts shoppers fascinated by the age-old charm, and has even led to an influx of new shops into this residential neighbourhood.

🕐 1200-2000 daily
🏠 No. 346, Jiaxing St., Da'an
📞 +886 2 8732 5321
f delicateantique

"The store often co-curate exhibitions with artists, which storekeepers would be happy to tell you more about. There's a story behind every item!"

– Chang Chieh

26 Chenjingkai Office
Map J, P.107

Chen Jing-kai is a graphic designer and art director who finds inspiration in the history of handmade shoes in Taiwan and aims to find a new niche for this declining industry. Working to find the ideal shape, structure and materials, he came up with a formula for a timeless design that is made to last. Customers are to choose the style, leather, colour, sole and shoe laces to their liking, shoes are then crafted by experienced shoemakers locally. Although there would be a two-month wait before your shoes are ready, you can first marvel at the understated beauty of Chen's designs through the prototypes displayed neatly in the store.

🕐 1600-2000 (Tu-Su)
🏠 No. 134, Tong'an St., Da'an
📞 +886 9 8373 3838
f ChenJingkai

"These made-to-order leather shoes with top design and craftsmanship will make for a collectible item."
– Hsin Tan, tan tan

27 The Town Crier
Map H, P.106

Adopting a general store concept from the West, The Town Crier fulfils the mission entrusted in its name by introducing the new and worthwhile to Taipei. Handpicked by owner Luke from around the world, the store carries homeware and personal care brands with practicality and sustainability embedded in their concept. The curated objects are also chosen for great manufacture quality or craftsmanship, outstanding product design and fine ingredients. Just ask Luke if you have any questions. He will be happy to tell you more about brand stories and usage.

🕐 1400–2100 (W–M)
🏠 1/F, No. 7, Ln. 76, Siwei Rd., Da'an
📞 +886 2 2707 0020
f theTOWNCRIERstore

"If you like industrial bins, brushes, enamel kitchenware, this is the shop to visit!"

– Alice Wang, Alice Wang Design

28 Good Cho's
Map J, P.107

Travel back to old Taipei at Forty-Four South Village. Nestled between the high-rise buildings of the cosmopolitan Xinyi District, the former military veteran housing complex has been preserved and repurposed into a hub of creative endeavours. One of the village's resident, Good Cho's, is a curated space for light meals and design goods. Have a relaxing breakfast, lunch or one of the city's best bagels, available in a little more than ten flavours, while admiring the quaint relics of the village's original residents. Every Sunday and every other Saturday, Good Cho's holds the Simple Market to showcase local produce, brands and music.

🕙 1000–2000 (M–F), 0900–1830 (Sa–Su)
🏠 No. 54, Songqin St., Xinyi 📞 +886 2 2758 2609
🔗 www.goodchos.com.tw 📎 Closes monthly first Mondays. Advance booking required.

"*The weekend market is well-curated, featuring the works of various creatives and craftsmen as well as mini exhibitions.*"

– Wang Ching-fu, Pinmo Design Studio

29 Eslite Spectrum Songyan Store

Map L, P.108

Launched within the Songshan Cultural Park in 2013, Eslite Spectrum, in addition to a bookstore, is an emporium of lifestyle goods, fashion items and local crafts. What's more, there are also cinema, performance theatre, exhibition space, restaurants and hotel, all housed in a building designed by master architect Toyo Ito. A testimony of the renowned bookstore chain's passion to bolster the local cultural scene, the Songyan store is a great starting point for those who wish to get to know what's new in the city.

🕐 1100-2200 daily
🏠 No. 88, Yanchang Rd., Xinyi
📞 +886 2 6636 5888
URL artevent.eslite.com

"This is probably one of the most interesting retail hubs in Taipei that carries select collections of locally designed and crafted goods."

– Grace Wang, VVG GROUP

30 Fuhe Bridge Flea Market

Map P, P.109

Perhaps Taipei most beloved destination for thrift shoppers, Fuhe Bridge Flea Market is an outdoor square with six lanes of up to 250 vendors selling secondhand junk. Don't think well-curated. Think boisterous chaos and a hotch-potch of metal, plastic and ceramics. Treasure hunt amongst antiques, knick-knacks, vintage Chinese records, paintings of unknown artists and the more practical gadgets, and you will always find curiosities that fascinate you at bargain prices. Remember there is little time for you think twice, as the best finds are usually snatched up before noon.

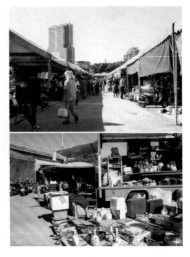

🕒 *0630–1200 (Sa–Su)*
🏠 *Fuhe Bridge, Yonghe, New Taipei City*

"The market closes at noon so be sure you go early!"
– Finger and Toe

31 Ri Xing Type Foundry
Map D, P.104

Chinese letterpress printing requires tens of thousands of moveable type characters. That's why when computerised printing emerged, the less efficient technique was deemed obsolete. Today, Ri Xing is the only running printer in Taiwan that still makes moveable types, and thus an important bastion of letterpress in Traditional Chinese. Upon visit, you will be mesmerised by the collection of 150,000 lead types that fills rows of slanted shelves in the store, which make for a unique memento. To preserve the craft, the foundry also organises occasional tours and workshops where you can see type casting in action.

🕐 0900–1200, 1330–1800 (M–F), 0930–1200, 1330–1700 (Sa) 🏠 No. 13, Ln. 97, Taiyuan Rd., Datong 📞 +886 2 2556 4626 **f** @rixingtypefoundry

"A living history of traditional Chinese letterpress."

– Yin Tsan-yu

32 Echo Store
Map L, P.108

Look for a giant bronze brush pen and a gourd-shaped door in the residential block off Bade Road, and you will find Echo Store. Created by notable sculptor Ju Ming, the brush pen was erected to commemorate Echo's publishing's new retail venture. Since 1971, Echo's publications have popularised science and passed on Chinese folklore to a generation of children. The store carries forward this mission by sourcing products made from folk arts like hand-dyeing, paper-cutting and book-binding. Of course, one can't miss the iconic publishing works by Echo, which study and document traditional culture and wisdom for the young.

🕑 1300–2000 (M–F), 1100–2000 (Sa)
🏠 No. 1, Aly. 16, Ln. 72, Sec. 4, Bade Rd., Songshan
📞 +886 2 2763 1452 (ext. 100–102)
🔗 www.hanshenggifts.com

"Home to a vanguard publisher in Taiwan which saw its heyday in the 1980s. The monumental children's encyclopedia was born here."

– Su Wei-hsiang, justfont

33 White Wabbit Records
Map G, P.105

White Wabbit is not just about records, it is about people. It was founded in 2002 by KK, the bassist of Aphasia, as a platform to introduce otherwise obscure band sounds to a larger audience. White Wabbit mainly focuses on independent music. Beside carrying records at the store, it is also a music agent and label of emerging local musicians. It also regularly invites underground bands from around the world to perform in Taiwan. If you are looking for something fresh or off the mainstream, this is the place for you. Also, staff here gives amazing recommendations.

🕐 1400–2200 daily
🏠 No. 1-1, Ln. 21, Pucheng St., Da'an
📞 +886 2 2369 7915
🔗 www.wwr.com.tw

"Feel free to listen to their records and find new tunes with the help of staff. Head to Shida Night Market and wander around the neighbourhood afterwards."
– Firstofmay studio

34 Nanmen Market
Map A, P.103

This traditional market has a 90-year-old history, dating back to when it was the main distribution centre for fruits and vegetables in Taipei during the Japanese colonial era. The present day Nanmen is homemaker's answer for groceries, dry and cooked food and deli – the Chinese version. Food lovers also flock here for specialty items. Zongzi, glutinous rice wrapped in bamboo leaves and traditional spices are some of the most sought after. The market is one of Taipei's best places to experience Chinese food culture, especially right before Lunar New Year – if you don't mind jam-packed spaces.

🕐 G-1/F Wet market, cooked food & grocery: 0700–1900, 2/F general merchandise: 1000–2200 daily
🏠 No. 8, Sec. 1, Roosevelt Rd., Zhongzheng
🔗 www.nanmenmarket.org.tw

"It's stunning to look at the meticulous displays of uzhou and Jiangzhe food stalls. You'll be dazzled just by the variety of dry-cured ham and cooked dishes."

– Ann Yu-chien

35 Yongle Fabric Market
Map B, P.103

Yongle is Taiwan's largest wholesale market for imported fabrics since Japanese occupation. Although textile manufacturing in fizzling out locally, the market remains vibrant as fashion designers and textile-related professionals' go-to place for the right fabric in mind. Browse countless imported or local designs on the first and second floor, some neatly displayed on shelves, some bunched up from inside the store and out the aisle. Many wholesalers are happy to work with individual customers. You can take your purchase to the tailors on the third floor. And grab a bite at the top floor food court, where Luc Besson's *Lucy* was filmed.

🕐 1000–1800 (M-Sa)
🏠 No. 21, Sec. 1, Dihua St., Datong

"The stunning sunset at Dadaocheng Wharf is just around the corner."

– Sim Chang

36 Jianguo Weekend Flower Market

Map C, P.103

Green thumbs and gardeners alike flock to this flower market for binge shopping every weekend. Right below Jianguo South Road over-pass at the Xinyi Road intersection, over 200 professional growers and plant vendors peddle beautiful Taiwanese orchids, bonsai, bamboo, and more for as little as NT$100. A great place to learn about Asian flora, you can also find seeds, gardening tools and garden furniture here. The most prized being those made from local camphor trees, which exude a unique fragrance that repels insects.

🕐 0900-1800 (Sa-Su)
📍 Sec. 1, Jiangguo S. Rd., Da'an
📞 +886 2 2702 6493
🔗 www.fafa.org.tw

"Arrive early to avoid leaving empty-handed."
— Committee of boys' day-off

Restaurants & Cafés

Savoury street eats, fresh local produce and curated coffee spaces

Simply put, Taipei is a foodie heaven. Exquisite presentation is not something you're looking for on the plate – you won't need it – but the wonderful flavours that come from fresh ingredients and ingenious cooking. With just NT$30 you will find yourself gnawing on a scrumptious bowl of braised pork rice or moreish oyster vermicelli noodles at the lively markets or anywhere on the street. If you come with a goal to try out the acclaimed Yong Kang Beef Noodle (*No. 17, Ln. 31, Sec. 2, Jinshan S. Rd., Da'an*) – one of Taiwanese culinary mainstays, be ready for a queue before you can slurp their damn good braised beef noodles served in Sichuan-style spicy red broth. For home-cooked meals at a more relaxing pace, try James Kitchen (#48) which distinguish itself for dallying with a great variety of quality local produce that has impressed international chefs alike. For the more inventive receipes, plan ahead for a sample of chef André's master creations at RAW Taipei (#39).

But of course Taipei is not just about savoury eats. Make it a routine to drink bubble tea or pick from a wide range of flavoured beverages available at every street corner. Alternatively, rest your legs and get your caffeine fix between meals at boutique cafés like Rufous (#44) and Fika Fika (*FB: @FikaFikaCafe*). In the meantime, teahouses continue to have a loyal following, with a young generation taking over the tradition to serve tea in equally modern and tranquil spaces. Among the burgeoning tea culture, Xiaoman Tea Experience (#38) is one of the top spots to enjoy a break.

mistroom
Graphic design studio

The designer duo enjoys wandering the lanes and through the woods, as well as the sounds of people and the city in the early hours. Together they run a studio with a small balcony.

Xiaoman Tea Experience
P.072

Ray Chen
Founder, Ray Chen International

Also the founder of Ray Chen + Partners Architects, Ray Chen is an architect and interior design. His work includes Taiwan's Eslite stores, Hotel Quote and cabin interior for China Airlines' Boeing 777-300ER fleet.

Page Tsou
Visual artist

Page Tsou completed a MA in Communication Art and Design at Royal College of Art in 2009 and now takes on both commercial and personal art projects.

Shi Yang
P.070

RAW
P.074

Sydney Sie
Visual artist

Sydney Sie combines illustration, photography, and motion graphics to create a two-dimensional world rife with gradient colours and representations of femininity.

Xiang Se
P.077

Blues To
Editor in chief, GQ Taiwan

Blues To's passion lies in living well and design aesthetics. With vast experience in lifestyle media, he seeks to bring new world visions to Taiwan and advances himself for a beautiful late life.

When Chen
Visual jockey & designer

When Chen creates for concerts. With a heart set on the 1970s, he collects old things and loves entertaining himself and everyone around him by playing the guitar.

About Animals
P.076

Le Park Cafe
P.078

Aaron Nieh
Graphic designer

Aaron Nieh focuses on Chinese pop albums and book designs. Recent work includes the visual branding of the 50th Taipei Golden Horse Film Festival and Tsai Ing-wen's election campaign.

Rufous Coffee
P.080

Ive Hu
Publisher, PPAPER

Ive Hu created PPAPER International, which publishes magazines that delves into the topics of culture, fashion, lifestyle and design.

Huang, Wei-jung
Creative director

Huang Wei-jung is a freelance creative director. Before that, has worked in advertising and wrote books. He was the founding editor-in-chief of magazines *Shopping Design* and *One Day*.

Solar Kitchen
P.079

Tsu Sheng Temple Food Stalls
P.082

Yao, Chung-han
Multimedia artist

Yao Chung-han teaches, creates and designs by day, and indulges in noises and dance music by night. He is a lecturer, a light and sound artist and electronic music composer.

Wistaria Tea House
P.084

22 Design Studio
Product design studio

Husband and wife Sean Yu and Yiting Cheng founded 22 Design Studio when they were 22 years old. Their work involves making accessories and stationery with cement.

Cheng, Tsung-lung
Artistic director, Cloud Gate 2

Cheng Tsung-lung started choreographing in 2002 and became Artistic Director of Cloud Gate 2 in 2014.

Hsiao's Wonton
P.083

James Kitchen
P.085

37 Shi Yang
Map X, P.111

Nestled deep in the lush mountains outside of Taipei, this ethereal teahouse has no fixed menu. Each meal offers up to ten courses of Chinese and Japanese fusion dishes, prepared with seasonal ingredients from the surrounding forest, as well as seafood fresh off the boat from Keelung, and guests can choose whether to go vegetarian. The experience will last for around three hours, and can be enjoyed while gazing out at framed views of the landscape on comfortable tatami mats.

🕐 1200–1500, 1800–2100 (Tu–Su) 💲 NT$1250
🏠 No. 5 & 7, Ln. 350, Sec. 3, Xiwan Rd.,
Xizhi, New Taipei City
📞 +886 2 2646 2266 🌐 www.shi-yang.com
🔗 1-week advance booking required for
weekday visits and 1.5 months for weekends.

"May is the month to enjoy the sight of tung tree flowers fluttering in the air like snow. At night, their staff may even take you to view fireflies at the rear of Shi Yang."

– mistroom

38 Xiaoman Tea Experience
Map G, P.105

Set up by tea whiz Xiaoman Hsieh, this teahouse embodies a notion of slowing down one's pace, which the name literally stands for. Lush greenery at its doorstep calms your nerves as you enter the establishment. Inside, elemental dark wood furniture and floral art spread over an ample space, oozing a calm and peaceful ambience. Roasted, unroasted, aged or young, the long list of teas served here are selected from Taiwan's independent tea farms by Xiaoman, with some varieties from China. Xiaoman also doubles as an events space, periodically showing works from Japanese florists, pottery artists and tea masters.

🕙 1000–1800 (Tu–Su)
🏠 No. 39, Ln. 16, Taishun St., Da'an
📞 +886 2 2365 0017 f xiaoman.tea

"*Feel the heartwarming vibe reminiscing old Taiwan as people are brought closer here.*"

– Ray Chen, Ray Chen International

 39 RAW
Map Z, P.111

With top chefs reinterpreting Taiwanese tastes and global flavours as a common goal, it's small wonder that reservations have been hard to come by since day one Michelin Star-chef André Chiang (P.088) opened RAW back in his hometown in 2014. A true culinary laboratory, RAW's open kitchen see chefs adhere to seasonal eating in harmony with the 24 solar terms in Chinese lunar calendar, creating dishes that impress both the taste buds and the eyes. Diners can expect traditional dishes prepared with western techniques, all paired with biodynamic wines.

🕐 1130–1430, 1800–2200 (W–Su)
🏠 No. 301, Lequn 3rd Rd., Zhongshan
📞 +886 2 8501 5800 URL www.raw.com.tw
🔗 Online booking required

"RAW creates a harmonic fusion between Taiwanese and French cuisine. That aside, try their French rye bread and specialty drinks."

– Page Tsou

40 About Animals

Map P, P.109

A short walk away from the Wanlong MRT station, this cosy eatery is known for its mission to promote animal rights through a delightful meat-free menu. Besides animals, founders Lin Na and Lu Shang-yu also care deeply about sustainability and ensure their ingredients are locally and ethically-sourced. Try for yourself how creative can vegan toppings be! Burgers, sandwiches and paninis are all served on freshly baked bread. About Animals also offers rice dishes, plenty of snack options and an impressive list of imported beers.

🕐 1500–2200 (Tu-Th), 1100–2230 (F-M)
🏠 No. 9, Ln. 1, Jinglong St., Wenshan
📞 +886 2 2935 3633 📘 aboutanimalszr
📎 Cash only

"They offer a 20% discount on burgers every Monday. My favourite is Wasabi Veggie Patty Burger."

– Sydney Sie

41 Xiang Se
Map A, P.103

Peeled off paint, mottled farm furniture and soft lighting, everything in Xiang Se seems to be in sync with the quaint apartment building it is housed in, with a touch of French country-side vibe. The European charm continues in the menu. Salads, pasta and meat dishes are exquisitely prepared both in terms of taste and plating. The chefs at Xiang Se enjoy experimenting with local flavours, as you tell by their standouts, that include the charcuterie plate of Shaoxing ham and the beef gnocchi made from Taiwanese sweet potatoes. Don't miss the brick-shaped canelé for dessert, which took head chef Zoe over a year to develop the recipe.

🕐 1800–2200 (W–Th), 1130–1500, 1800–2200 (F–Sa), 1130–2200 (Su)
🏠 No. 1–2, Hukou St., Zhongzheng
📞 +886 2 2358 1819　f xiangse　✐ Aged 8+

"Quiet old flat meets southern France farmhouse. It's an ideal place for an afternoon tea break."

– Blues To, GQ Taiwan

 42 **Le Park Cafe**
Map E, P.104

Set in a former pediatric clinic, Le Park is
filled with the old world charm of an Italian
café. Opening the café fresh out of college,
owner Wen commissioned a woodworking
team from Tainan to handcraft seats and bar
space to match the anachronistic ambiance
the interior offers. Head upstairs for a quiet
break or a long chat with friends. Le Park uses
Caffe Trombetta beans. Served hot or with
ice, mocha is one of patrons' favourite. The
word is also spreading about their caramel
cappuccino, excellent apple pies and black
sugar-coated crème brûlée.

🕐 1300-2300 (W-M)
🏠 No. 146, Liaoning St., Zhongshan
📞 +886 2 2719 8880   📘 Le park cafe
💳 Cash only

*"Love the old house, vintage furniture, banana cake
and apple pie à la mode."*
– When Chen

43 Solar Kitchen

Map I, P.107

Solar Kitchen in the popular Fujin Street area is an advocate of healthy cooking with locally-sourced ingredients. Organic, fair trade and no artificial additives are some values the restaurant uphold for the sake of diners and also mother earth. Primarily European, the seasonal menu sometimes gets creative and fuses Taiwanese flavours with excellent outcome. No matter the dish, the Kitchen always makes a point of educating each diner about the ingredients used. Home chefs, or those interested in chatting with local suppliers can also check out the farmers market hosted here each weekend.

1130–2130 (Th–Tu)
No. 421, Fujin St., Songshan
+886 2 2767 6211 *@SolarKitchen.tw*
URL *shop.solarkitchen.tw*

"A little pricey but worth a try. Apart from savoury dishes, the restaurant also offers winning bread and desserts."

– Aaron Nieh

44 Rufous Coffee
Map K, P.107

At the heart of Rufous is Xiaoyang, a skilled barista whose unique house blend earned him an impressive 91 point score from Coffee Review. Since its opening in 2007, Rufous has become known for its innovative coffee menu. Iced hops coffee, cognac espresso are just two of its popular endeavours. Those who are looking for something regular will also enjoy its smooth hazelnut latte. Moved recently to a more spacious location next to its original address, the same dim light and curiosity-decked wooden fixtures make patrons comfortable for a relaxing stay. Roasting all of its beans in-house, the aroma only makes coffee lovers linger longer in the café.

🕐 1300-2200 (F-W)
🏠 No. 339, Sec. 2, Fuxin S. Rd., Da'an
📞 +886 2 2736 6880
f RUFOUS COFFEE

"A meeting place for the sophisticated, it brews authentic ice drip coffee as rich and mellow as fine wine."

– Ive Hu, PPAPER

45 Tsu Sheng Temple Food Stalls
Map B, P.103

Cheap eats at Tsu Sheng Temple's public square used to be a working class relish, but the delectable tastes later draw people from all walks of life. Pick from more than 20 vendors at once and enjoy assorted dishes under banyan trees with the local community – eating al fresco against the heat at public squares is part of Taiwan's unique temple culture. It can get really hot in summer, but you can always cool it down with a cold beer or two. Come early as popular dishes such as pork knuckle noodles and spare ribs and turnip soup usually sells out before noon.

🕘 0900-1700 daily
🏠 No. 17, Ln. 49, Bao'an St., Datong

"Go with at least three friends so you can sample a wide variety of dishes. Order something from different stalls. The owners will take the food to you when it's ready."
– Huang Wei-jung

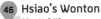

46 Hsiao's Wonton
Map U, P.110

Savoury rice balls, fish ball soup, and wontons are the classic comfort food at Hsiao's that consistently draws large crowds every morning starting at around 7am. Slightly larger than the Guangzhou variety, Hsiao's wontons are generously filled with seasoned minced pork, the same goes to their fish balls, which are juicy at each bite. Order rice balls if you are looking for a more filling option. A little bit of sweet sauce and garlic mash goes well with its glutinous texture. The menu is in Chinese only, but don't hesitate to ask for help. Also, get here early, as they frequently sell out by noon.

🕐 0700–1600 (Tu–F), –1400 (Sa–Su)
🏠 No. 21, Ln. 40, Yumin 1st Rd., Beitou
📞 +886 2 2822 4837

"Fresh rice balls are made daily and sell out fast. Go early or regret it!"
– Yao Chung-han

47 Wistaria Tea House
Map G, P.105

Named after the century-old wistaria tree that has stood outside since construction, the former residence of a Japanese high official had once lived as an intellectual hotbed for democratic activism after economist Zhou De-wei moved in during the 1950s. It was not opened to public until the 1980s, and has quickly grown into an enclave for artists and cultural critics. Enter through the well-maintained garden into the teahouse where you can order from a wide range of teas, all aptly described in the extensive menu. The waitstaff will demonstrate tea-drinking custom before you are encouraged to try it yourself.

🕐 1000-2200 daily
🏠 No. 1, Ln. 16, Sec. 3, Xinsheng S. Rd. Da'an
📞 +886 2 2363 7375 URL wistariateahouse.com

"Their green bean pastry is one of our favourites! Reservation is recommended."

– Sean Yu & Yiting Cheng, 22 Design Studio

48 James Kitchen

Map G, P.105

On the south end of Yongkang Street is James Kitchen, a pair of cosy neighbourhood restaurants occupying two separate street addresses. Founded in 2005 by the now-retired James Tseng, the original restaurant with only four tables was well-loved by local foodies for its authentic Taiwanese fare. The second unit followed with a selection of creatively-presented dishes influenced by Central-Taiwanese family cooking. These simple, comforting dishes include fried fresh oyster roll, radish omelet, and pork-fat rice. Dining here can strike a nostalgic chord, and the food is unforgettable.

🕐 Store 1: 1130-1400, 1700-2200 daily, Store 2: 1730-0000 (Tu-Su)
🏠 1/F, No. 42-5 & 65, Yongkang St., Da'an
📞 +886 2 2358 2393, +886 2 2343 2275
📘 peterkitchentaipei   🔗 Cash only

"These interesting Taiwanese restaurants only use the freshest ingredients."
– Cheng Tsung-lung, Cloud Gate 2

烤生蠔

烤活蝦

草蝦 竹身烤
900/斤
900/斤

Nightlife

Locally-brewed beers, night markets and live music venues

Taipei is indeed a city for night owls! One can hit up clubs and music venues until dawn, eat local delicacies at the many night markets until stuffed, or enjoy the night view on Yangmingshan. The eastern part of the city is packed with bars and clubs but do dig out smaller venues hidden in residential districts. Frequented by locals, these are usually where you will feel most connected to the city. Among them, Fucking Place (*2/F, No. 169, Sec. 2, Heping E. Rd., Da'an*) is a great start. Some leading nightclubs work with visual artists to create mesmerising motion graphics in sync with music. Such immersive experience can be enjoyed at OMNI (#53) or Korner (*FB: @Kornertw*), which focuses on electronic beats by top DJs.

While large shows are staged at Taipei Arena, Taiwan's concert culture is defined by smaller-scale performances. From the mid-size Legacy Taipei (#54) with a 1,200 capacity, to Riverside Music Cafe (*B2, Ln. 244, Sec. 3, Roosevelt Rd., Zhongzheng*) with a room for a little more than 100 audience, both established and up-and-coming musicians can get close to their audience with their music.

Although it is a bit of a cliché to talk about which night market offers the best eats, extending your food trip into the zero hours is a quintessential Taipei experience. As the golden rule goes: the longer the line, the better the food!

Revolver
P.091

nos:books
Publisher

Cherng
Illustrator

Cherng has made Taipei home for some 20 years where he shares his insights into life through illustrations. He is a right-hander but he draws with his left hand.

HOUTH
Branding studio

nos:books publishes limited releases that realise ideas and concepts for local and overseas artists. They run an online shop, and participate in book fairs from time to time.

Chuoyinshi
P.090

Behind HOUTH, illustrator Ho Wan-chun and photographer Huang Chi-teng work in hands to integrate creativity, design, illustration and visual graphics into fresh solutions.

Xiaozhang's Seafood
P.092

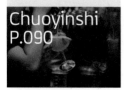

haoshi design
Product design studio

OMNI
P.094

Liu, Keng-ming
Founder, Bito

Literally equivalent to "good thing" in Chinese, haoshi discovers goodness in life. The studio instills purity and peace into designs to free users from disarray in life.

André Chiang
Chef

Liu Keng-ming started off as a director, designer and illustrator in New York. He later returned and pursue motion design in Taiwan, believing it a key graphic design for the next generation.

The Top
P.093

My roots in southern French nouvelle cuisine influences both my lifestyle and cooking. I use only fresh artisan produce and now helm the RAW and Restaurant André teams.

Legacy Taipei
P.095

Raykai Chen
Vocalist, 1976 & Kafka by the Sea

1976 was named the Best Band by the 21st Golden Melody Awards in Taiwan. Raykai Chen also founded music label re: public records and runs multi-purpose venue, Kafka by the Sea.

Ounce
P.097

Richie Lin
Chef, MUME

Having worked at Noma in Copenhagen and Quay in Sydney, Hong Kong-born Chef Richie Lin opened MUME and gets creative with Taiwanese produce.

Jeffrey Wang
Founder, BLANQ

I've lived my life between New York and Asia. I started branding and creative agency, BLANQ, which mainly focuses on hotel, development, restaurant and fashion industries.

Kafka by the Sea
P.096

East End
P.098

Spencer Chou
Founder, boven magazine library

Having lived the good old days when music and books are in high demand, Spencer Chou focuses his efforts on revolutionising reading habits in Taiwan in the years to come.

Nanjichang
Night Market
P.100

Tom Lin
Director & screenwriter

Raised in the US and Taiwan, Tom Lin seeks to balance Western narratives and Eastern meditation in his work. He started working in film after earning his MFA at California Institute of the Arts.

Cosmos People
Band

Formed in the summer of 2004, the trio who met at Jianguo High School roams the earth to document the lives of today's youth through music.

Double
Check
P.099

Raohe Street
Night Market
P.101

49 Chuoyinshi
Map L, P.108

It is difficult to find a seat at Chuoyinshi on a Friday or Saturday, but that's part of its charm. Standing with strangers in a packed room is the ultimate way to taste the bar's rich selections of imported craft beers picked by the five inventive beer lovers who also founded Taiwan's premium boutique microbrewery, Taihu Brewing. Choose from a daily changing menu of more than 20 craft beers from around the world on tap including Taihu's own creations. Come before 6pm if you desperately need to sit.

🕐 1700-2330 (M-Th), 1500-0130 (F-Sa), 1500- (Su)
🏠 Chuoyinshi Landmark: No. 68, Sec. 5,
Zhongxiao E. Rd., Xinyi   📞 +886 2 2722 0592
📘 @cysxinyi

"You can try them all until you find your favourite!"
– Cherng

50 Revolver
Map A, P.103

One can't visit Revolver without eyeing the sign "No Coldplay". It's nothing personal – co-owner Jeremy Gray simply wishes to introduce a diverse spectrum of independent music to the Taipei crowd – anything but pop music that the band represents. With a cosy setting and a spacious storefront for meet and greet, its ground floor bar offers patrons a wide range of beverages including local and imported craft beers at NT$80-150 during happy hours. One floor up is a sizable livehouse that set the stage for alternative rock, punk and DJ gigs every night. The convivial happenings attract music lovers, drinkers and expats from all over Taipei.

🕐 1830-0300 (M-Th), -0500 (F-Sa), 1800-0100 (Su)
🏠 No.1-1, Sec. 1, Roosevelt Rd., Zhongzheng
📞 +886 2 3393 1678 URL www.revolver.tw

"Happy hours run from 6.30 to 9.30pm nightly. Get some fixed-priced Taiwanese draft beer instead if you arrive late."

– HOUTH

51 Xiaozhang's Seafood
Map E, P.104

Fresh seafood is not a rare find here – the trick is singling out the best quality among daily catches and spot what is in season. That being said, Xiaozhang's is the local joint to visit. Former fisherman named by his surname Zhang takes pride in commuting early each morning to the port of Yilan just to bring back the finest of that day's catch. Have them raw, steamed or deep fried. Their dishes are simply prepared with just a dash of seasoning to bring out the ingredients' original flavours. Be sure to try the shrimp fried rice, deep fried codling, or Mr Zhang's homemade fish soup, and ask the waitstaff for some rare varieties as well.

🕐 1700-0100 daily
🏠 No. 73, Liaoning St., Zhongshan
📞 +886 9 2780 8693

"Pre-order shrimp sashimi. They sell out really quickly."
– nos:books

52 The Top
Map T, P.110

Set atop of Yangming Mountain, The Top with
its terraced setting offers patrons the most
stunning view of Taipei city that spans from
Taipei 101 all the way to Banqiao District. Tropical
greenery and cool-toned ambient lighting
make for a unique atmosphere that is both laid
back and glamorous. From modular sofas to
private pavilions, seating areas are ample and
as diverse as the menu offerings, making it an
ideal choice for large groups. Bookings are only
available for private booths, which requires
with a minimum spending of NT$3,000 to
NT$8,000. Groups of seven or less should come
as early as 4pm at weekends to snag a table.

🕐 1700-0300 (M-Th), -0500 (F), 1200-0500 (Sa),
1200- (Su)
📍 No. 33, Aly. 4, Ln. 61, Kaixuan Rd., Shilin
📞 +886 2 2862 2255 URL www.compei.com

*"Whether it is dusk time or dark when the city's
flooded with neon lights, Yangming Mountain always
offers the best view of the city."*

– haoshi design

53 OMNI
Map H, P.106

Taking over the one-time home of Taipei's legendary club Luxy in 2015, OMNI sustains the storied legacy that its former occupant left behind. Dynamic special effects and lighting, state-of-the-art sound system, and a panoramic curved LED screen that wraps around the massive open dance floor synchronise to dazzle patrons with an immersive sound and visual experience. Party at this winner of 2016's iF Design Award and be mesmerised by multimedia shows and the cutting edge art direction and production efforts that put Taipei's nightlife on the map.

🕐 2230-0430 (W, F-Sa)
🏠 5/F, No. 201, Sec. 4, Zhongxiao E. Rd., Da'an
📞 +886 9 8380 3388
URL www.omni-taipei.com

"I'd say it is the best nightclub in Taiwan. Just chill, relax and have fun there!"
– André Chiang, RAW Taipei & Restaurant André

54 Legacy Taipei
Map F, P.105

Attend a concert at Legacy Taipei for an inside glimpse of Taipei's thriving music culture. With a capacity of up to 1,200 music fans, this medium-sized venue has always been a favourite for indie bands looking for a larger stage and pop figures who wish to greet fans in a more intimate setting. Since 2009, Legacy has attracted a loyal and spirited local crowd and in turn contributes to bringing Taipei's livehouse culture to the mainstream. The musical hub's premier acoustics also make it a top choice for international artists like Dir en grey, St. Vincent and James Blake.

🏠 Huashan 1914 Creative Park, No. 1, Sec. 1, Bade Rd., Zhongzheng   📞 +886 2 2395 6660
🔗 www.legacy.com.tw
🎫 Tickets are available at www.indievox.com, or on site two hours before show opens (cash only).

"The screams, bottled beers and the space remind me of the days I spent watching gigs in Brooklyn's garages. So much energy flows in this place!"

– Liu Keng-ming, Bito

55 Kafka by the Sea
Map O, P.109

Just a stone's throw from National Taiwan University, Kafka by the Sea is a café by day, and a live house by night. Music is everything here between the artist and their audience, where live performances are often lined up at weekends, with an inclination to acoustic music. The café serves light meals besides coffee, and dedicates a corner to books and albums for sale near the entrance. If you're in luck, you might be looking at the next big thing making his/her debuts or household names playing a simple, intimate gig.

🕐 1130–2230 (M–Th), 1200–0000 (F–Su)
🏠 2/F, No. 2, Ln. 244, Sec. 3, Roosevelt Rd., Zhongzheng
📞 +886 2 2364 1996 📘 @kafka.republic

"Come for a good cup of coffee and stay for a show!"
– Raykai Chen, 1976 & Kafka by the Sea

56 Ounce
Map J, P.107

Dim light, dark wood furnishings and intimate seating – Ounce fully revitalises America's speakeasy halfway around the world. Find the right doorknob on a secret door inside a homely café, and you will enter the world of creative mixology. More than suiting your preference, the bar's upscale cocktails were all made-to-order to give pleasant surprises. The hangout has now ventured into food, offering gourmet dinner and cocktail pairing as Ounce+PLUS until they find another permanent home. Meanwhile, Ounce is also actively bringing about new collaborations. The first being a drinks and haircut pop-up with Taiwan's BIBA Salon.

🕑 Check for pop-up events on Facebook
🏠 No. 40, Ln. 63, Sec. 2, Dunhua S. Rd., Da'an
📞 +886 2 2708 6755
f @OunceTaipei
🔗 Ounce+PLUS: 1700-2200 (M-Sa)

"This is arguably the best speakeasy bar in Taipei. Their cocktails are always amazing!"

– Richie Lin, MUME

57 **East End**
Map H, P.106

Residing in Hotel Proverbs, a sleek establishment designed by Taiwanese starchitect Ray
Chen (P.068), East End stands out not only due to
its industrial-glam interior, but also to the sheer
creative energy of Japanese mixologist and
co-founder Hidetsugu Ueno, who fuses local
ingredients like winter melon and longan into
world-class cocktails. One of the best drinks
include the Emerald, a take on James Bond's
favourite Vesper Martini, which combines Taiwanese green tea with London dry gin. The bar
also has a vast outdoor terrace, a place to enjoy
cigars and cocktails above the busy streetscape
three floors below.

🕐 1400-0100 (Su-Th), -0200 (F-Sa)
🏠 3/F, Hotel Proverbs, No. 56, Sec. 1, Da'an Rd., Da'an
📞 +886 9 0353 1851   f @EASTENDBARTAIPEI

*"East End has the most refined cocktails in town
and you can savour the amount of effort they put
into the drink every single sip you take."*
– Jeffrey Wang, BLANQ

58 Double Check
Map H, P.106

Take your shoes off at the door and get ready for a memorable night at owner and resident DJ Ken's music lounge. Envisioned as a near perfect chic living lounge, Double Check adopts a no-shoe policy to make you feel at home. House rule aside, the menu is kept minimal, but visitors will be pleased with their beer, wine and whiskey options along with a curated playlist on loop through their FOCAL sound system. A great choice of music magazines and most importantly a stellar guest DJ line-up also make Double Check a to-go spot for fans of the mixed sounds.

🕐 1700–0000 (Su–Th), –0100 (F–Sa)
🏠 1/F, No. 16, Aly. 5, Ln. 107, Sec. 1, Fuxin S. Rd., Da'an
📞 +886 2 2778 3385
📘 @doublecheck.tw

"*Don't miss live DJ sounds on Wednesday, Friday and Saturday nights.*"

– Spencer Chou, boven magazine library

59 Nanjichang Night Market
Map A, P.102

This is how the locals call it – "south airport".
Hidden in Wanhua District, Nanjichang Night
Market sits next to a former military airfield
south of Songshan Airport that operated during
Japanese occupation. Still one of Taipei's best
kept secret, this small market offers nothing
fancy but guaranteed authentic taste. The pork
and chive dumplings are a great start, so as the
sizzling Shanghai-style pan-fried buns and the
crispy fried chicken. Historic apartment blocks
with iconic spiral staircases overlook the market, adding to its enchanting old Taipei vibe.

🕐 1600–0000 daily
🏠 Sec. 2, Zhonghua Rd., Wanhua

*"Many stands haven't changed a bit for the last 20
years in favour with foreigners. A visit to the market
will make you feel like walking into a time capsule."*
– Tom Lin

60 Raohe Street Night Market
Map N, P.108

Flashing LED signs in this bustling 250 year-old temple complex make the night market a scene straight out of Ridley Scott's Blade Runner. Started off as one of Taipei's first public markets, Raohe has become known for its diverse street eats as well as fashionable clothing and goodies at bargain prices, which bring tourists and locals alike to find great treats in this 600-metre long street. Simply embrace the chaos, get lost, eat and shop your way out. While most food stall signs are in Chinese, language is not a problem at all – just follow the long queues for the best bites.

🕑 1700-2300 daily
🏠 Raohe St., Songshan

"Go there by MRT or YouBike. Eat, drink, shop, play and be merry."
– Cosmos People

MAP A

Feng Da Coffee ●
15
⊘ Ximen
● Top Coffee Ho

Ah Cai Milkfish ●
NEIJIANG ST

BO'AI RD

Presidential Office
Building ●

SEC 2 CHANGSHA ST

XINING S RD

SEC 1 ZHONGHUA RD

SEC 2 GUIYANG ST

SEC 1 GUIYANG ST

KANGDING RD

GUILIN RD

2

BO'AI RD

● Wanhua Herb Alloy

AIGUO W RD

GUANGZHOU ST

⊘ Xiaonann

⊘ Longshan
Temple
SEC 3 HEPING W RD

BO'AI RD

🕉 Wanhua
BANGKA BLVD
Shimokitazawa Books ●

**TAIPEI
BOTANICAL
GARDEN**
6
National
Craft Resear
Development in

WANDA RD

JUGUANG RD

National Museum
of History ●

SEC 2 HEPING W RD
N

XIZANG RD
HU'AN ST
59

....

● 2_Lungshan Temple
● 6_Taipei Botanical Garden
● 15_The Red House
● 59_Nanjichang Night Market

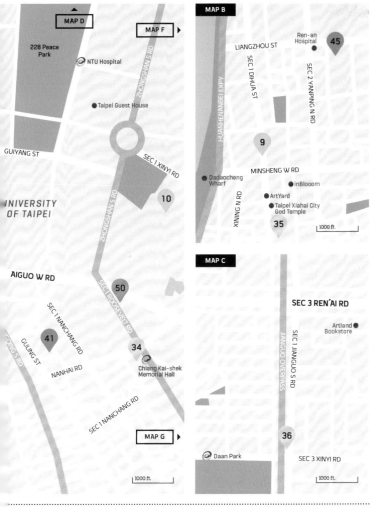

- 9_Dihua Street
- 10_National Theater and Concert Hall
- 34_Nanmen Market
- 35_Yongle Fabric Market
- 36_Jianguo Weekend Flower Market
- 41_Xiang Se
- 45_Tsu Sheng Temple Food Stalls
- 50_Revolver

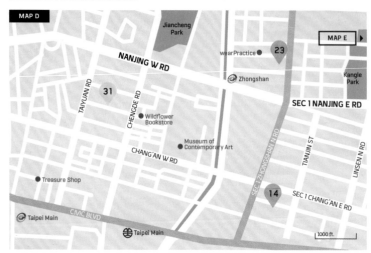

- 14_Pon Ding
- 22_Suho Memorial Paper Museum
- 23_SPOT Taipei
- 31_Ri Xing Type Foundry
- 42_Le Park Cafe
- 51_Xiaozhang's Seafood

- 7_Qidong Street Japanese Houses
- 24_Huashan 1914 Creative Park
- 33_White Wabbit Records
- 38_Xiaoman Tea Experience
- 47_Wistaria Tea House
- 48_James Kitchen
- 54_Legacy Taipei

MAP H

MAP L ▶

- ● 13_boven magazine library
- ● 27_The Town Crier
- ● 53_OMNI
- ● 57_East End
- ● 58_Double Check

- 5_Koo Chen-fu Memorial Library
- 20_transpark
- 25_Delicate Antique
- 26_Chenjingkai Office
- 28_Good Cho's
- 43_Solar Kitchen
- 44_Rufous Coffee
- 56_Ounce

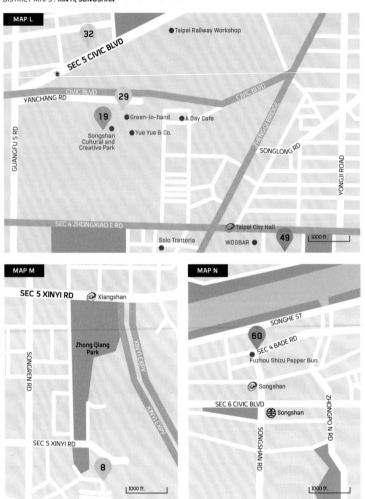

MAP L

32

SEC 5 CIVIC BLVD

Taipei Railway Workshop

CIVIC BLVD

YANCHANG RD

29

CIVIC BLVD

ZHONGXIAO BRIDGE

GUANGFU S RD

19

Green-in-hand

A Day Cafe

Yue Yue & Co.

Songshan Cultural and Creative Park

SONGLONG RD

YONGJI ROAD

SEC 4 ZHONGXIAO E RD

Taipei City Hall

Solo Trattoria

WOOBAR

49

1000 ft.

MAP M

SEC 5 XINYI RD

Xiangshan

Zhong Qiang Park

XINYI EXPY

XINYI EXPY

SONGREN RD

SEC 5 XINYI RD

8

1000 ft.

MAP N

SONGHE ST

60

SEC 4 BADE RD

Fuzhou Shizu Pepper Bun

Songshan

SEC 6 CIVIC BLVD

Songshan

SONGSHAN RD

ZHONGPO N RD

1000 ft.

- 8_Elephant Mountain Hiking Trail
- 19_Not Just Library
- 29_Eslite Spectrum Songyan Store
- 32_Echo Store
- 49_Chuoyinshi
- 60_Raohe Street Night Market

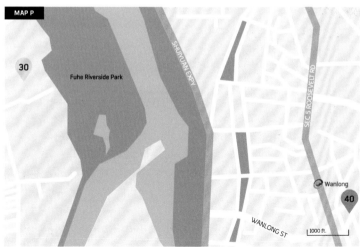

- 4_Treasure Hill
- 30_Fuhe Bridge Flea Market
- 40_About Animals
- 55_Kafka by the Sea

DISTRICT MAPS : BEITOU, SHILIN, TAMSUI (NEW TAIPEI CITY)

MAP Q

21
Taiwan Golf & Country Club
Huwei Fort ●
SEC 1 ZHONGZHENG RD
1000 ft.

MAP R

ZHONGHE ST
QUANYUAN RD
Xinbeitou
ZHONGSHAN RD
GUANGMING RD
11
Beitou Hot Spring Museum ●
1000 ft.

MAP S

QUANYUAN RD
Marshal Zen Garden ●
16
Thermal Valley ●
1000 ft.

MAP T

Chinese Culture University ●
GUANGHUA RD
52
1000 ft.

MAP U

YUMIN 2ND RD
46
ZHENHUA ST
SEC 1 DONGHUA ST
Shipai
YUMIN 6TH RD
1000 ft.

MAP V

1
Zhishan Garden
SEC 2 ZHISHAN RD
1000 ft.

- ● 1_National Palace Museum
- ● 11_Beitou Public Library
- ● 16_Beitou Museum
- ● 21_Cloud Gate Theater
- ● 46_Hsiao's Wonton
- ● 52_The Top

- 3_College of Design @Shih Chien University
- 12_Taipei Riverside Bikeways
- 17_siu siu: Lab of Primitive Senses
- 18_Xue Xue Institute
- 37_Shi Yang
- 39_RAW

Accommodation

Hip hostels, fully-equipped apartments & swanky hotels

No journey is perfect without a good night's sleep to recharge. Whether you're backpacking or on a business trip, our picks combine top quality and convenience, whatever your budget.

 < NT$2000   NT$2001–4000

 NT$4001–8000

NiHao Cafe Hotel

Hidden in a quiet alley just three minutes' walk from Da'an station, NiHao greets guests with a lush patio. The hotel's double to family rooms are exquisite, well-equipped and decked with leafy potted plants to set a convivial mood. The café offers scrumptious breakfast and lunch to guests at 15% off. Also try the daily fresh pastries, which have built a loyal fan base.

🏠 *No. 4, Aly. 5, Ln. 147, Sec. 3, Xinyi Rd, Da'an*
📞 *+886 2 2389 7563*
📘 *nihaocafehotel*

Play Design Hotel

Play Design encourages design-conscious travellers to use, sleep in and shop the works of some 100 designer brands from Taiwan. Experience local culture, creativity, craft and manufacturing technology firsthand in the five themed rooms. One can also curate their own room by arranging furnishings on the website.

🏠 No.156-2 Taiyuan Road, Datong 📞 +886 2 2555 5930 URL www.playdesignhotel.com Ⓢ

Folio Da'an

🏠 No. 23, Ln. 30, Sec. 4, Xinyi Rd., Da'an
📞 +886 2 6626 0658
URL www.folio-hotels.com/daan

Roaders Hotel

🏠 No. 68, Yanping S. Rd., Zhongzheng
📞 +886 2 2312 0589
URL www.roadershotel.com

9Floor Apt.

URL www.9floorspace.com

Art'otel Ximending

🏠 No. 124–2, Sec. 2, Wuchang St., Wanhua
📞 +886 2 2388 5558
f artoteltaipei

SWIIO Da'an

🏠 No. 185, Sec. 1, Da'an Rd., Da'an
📞 +886 2 2703 2220
URL www.swiio.com

Notes

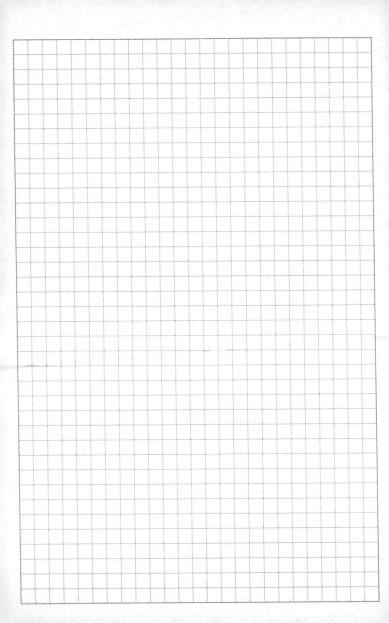

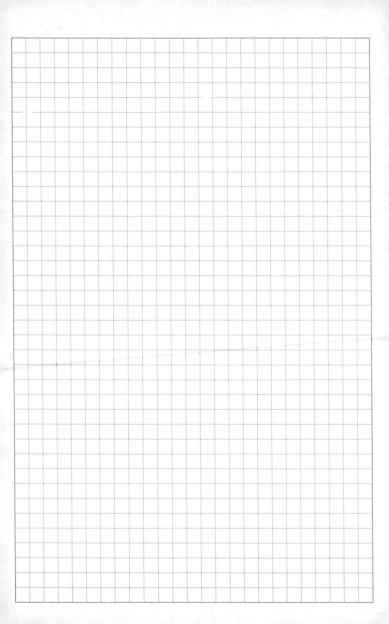

Index

Multimedia

Chou Tung-yen @Very Mainstream Studio, *p034*
FB: Chou Tung-yen
Portrait by Li Xin-zhe

Finger and Toe, *p058*
cargocollective.com/fingerand-toe

Johnason Lo @JL Design, *p045*
www.jldesign.tv

Liu Keng-ming @Bito, *p095*
www.bito.tv

Muh Chen @Grass Jelly, *p015*
www.grassjelly.tv

When Chen, *p078*
whenchen.com

Yao Chung-han, *p083*
www.yaolouk.com

Music

Cosmos People, *p101*
FB: @cosmospeople

Firstofmay studio, *p062*
FB: @firstofmaystudio

Raykai Chen @1976 & Kafka by the Sea, *p096*
www.the1976.com
FB: @kafka.republic

Riin @The Girl and The Robots, *p022*
FB: the.girl.and.the.robots

Photography

Chang Chieh, *p050*
www.behance.net/changchieh0123/

Kair Chen, *p023*
www.cargocollective.com/KairChen

Sim Chang, *p064*
www.sim.tw

Sydney Sie, *p076*
sydneysie.com

Publishing

Blues To @GQ Taiwan, *p077*
www.gq.com.tw

Committee of boys' day-off, *p065*
FB: @dayoff.daily

Huang Wei-jung , *p082*
FB: @esliteonthedesk

Ive Hu @PPAPER, *p080*
FB: ivehu

nos:books, *p092*
nosbooks.com

Photo & other credits

Chuoyinshi, *p090*
(All) Chuoyinshi

Cloud Gate Theater, *p041*
(p028, p041 Interior & Dance)
Liu Zhen-xiang

Legacy Taipei, *p095*
(Band shows) Legacy Taipei

National Theater and Concert Hall, *p024–025*
(p024) Xu Bin (p025) Chen Min-jia

OMNI, *p094*
(All) Derek

Ounce, *p097*
(All) Ounce

RAW Taipei, *p074–075*
(All) RAW Taipei

Shi Yang, *p70–p071*
(p066 & p070-071 All) Shi Yang

SPOT Taipei, *p044*
(All) The Taipei House

The Red House, *p034*
(All) The Red House

In Accommodation: all courtesy of respective hotels. NiHao Cafe Hotel, by motif.com.tw

CITIX60

CITIx60: Taipei

First published and distributed by
viction workshop ltd

viction:ary™

7C Seabright Plaza, 9-23 Shell Street,
North Point, Hong Kong

Url: www.victionary.com
Email: we@victionary.com
🅵 @victionworkshop
🐦 @victionary_
📷 @victionworkshop

Edited and produced by viction:ary

Concept & art direction: Victor Cheung
Research & editorial: Caroline Kong, Queenie Ho
Coordination: Katherine Wong
Design & map illustration: MW Wong, Frank Lo

Project management: UN1 INC.
Contributing writer: Emma Karasz
Cover map illustration: Whooli Chen
Count to 10 illustrations: Guillaume Kashima aka Funny Fun
Photography: TODAY TODAY

Content is compiled based on facts available as of March 2017. Travellers are
advised to check for updates from respective locations before your visit.

First edition
978-988-77746-1-7
Printed and bound in China

Acknowledgements

A special thank you to all creatives, photographer(s), editor, producers, companies and organisations for your crucial contributions to our inspiration and
knowledge necessary for the creation of this book. And, to the many whose
names are not credited but have participated in the completion of the book,
we thank you for your input and continuous support all along.

CITIX60
City Guides

CITIx60 is a handpicked list of hot spots that illustrates the spirit of the world's most exhilarating design hubs. From what you see to where you stay, this city guide series leads you to experience the best — the places that only passionate insiders know and go.

Each volume is a unique collaboration with local creatives from selected cities. Known for their accomplishments in fields as varied as advertising, architecture and graphics, fashion, industry and food, music and publishing, these locals are at the cutting edge of what's on and when. Whether it's a one-day stopover or a longer trip, **CITIx60** is your inspirational guide.

Stay tuned for new editions.

City guides available now:

Amsterdam
Barcelona
Berlin
Copenhagen
Hong Kong
Istanbul
Lisbon
London
Los Angeles
Milan
Melbourne
New York
Paris
Portland
Singapore
Stockholm
Taipei
Tokyo
Vancouver
Vienna